Be Smart About Money

S0-EIG-931

Money Management and Budgeting

Sherri Mabry Gordon

BE SMART
ABOUT
MONEY
AND
FINANCIAL
LITERACY

Enslow Publishers, Inc
40 Industrial Road
Box 398
Berkeley Heights, NJ 07922
USA

http://www.enslow.com

Library of Congress Cataloging-in-Publication Data

Gordon, Sherri Mabry.
  Be smart about money : money management and budgeting / Sherri Mabry Gordon.
    pages cm. — (Be smart about money and financial literacy)
  Includes index.
  Summary: "Examines money management and budgeting, including saving and spending strategies, making decisions about the best financial products and services, and creating a personal budget"—Provided by publisher.
  Audience: Grade 9 to 12.
  ISBN 978-0-7660-4292-6
  1. Finance, Personal—Juvenile literature. 2. Budgets, Personal—Juvenile literature. 3. Financial literacy—Juvenile literature. I. Title.
  HG179.G6925 2014
  332.024—dc23

                        2013006119

Future editions:
Paperback ISBN: 978-1-4644-0529-7
EPUB ISBN: 978-1-4645-1270-4
Single-User PDF ISBN: 978-1-4646-1270-1
Multi-User PDF ISBN: 978-0-7660-5903-0

Printed in the United States of America

112013 Bang Printing, Brainerd, Minn.

10 9 8 7 6 5 4 3 2 1

Enslow Publishers, Inc., is committed to printing our books on recycled paper. The paper in every book contains 10% to 30% post-consumer waste (PCW). The cover board on the outside of each book contains 100% PCW. Our goal is to do our part to help young people and the environment too!

Clipart Credits: Shutterstock.com.

Cover Illustration: Shutterstock.com (Benjamin Franklin) and © iStockphoto.com / Amanda Rohde (colonial suit).

Contents

Throughout the book, look for this logo 🖲 for smart financial tips and this logo 🖲 for bad choices to avoid. Also, don't forget to "Do the Math" at the end of each chapter.

Money Matters

Your first experience with managing money probably involved a piggy bank. Did you ever wonder why banks are shaped like pigs? After all, pigs aren't animals known to save like squirrels save nuts or dogs bury bones.

Well, according to history buffs, in the 1600s, it was common to store money in orange clay pots called "pyggs." As time passed, potters eventually started shaping these pots into pig shapes because the "pygg" name made people think of the farm animal. Thus, the first piggy banks were born in the 1700s.

Today, people still use piggy banks to store spare change. You might have one of your own. But now you're looking for more sophisticated ways to save and manage money. You may even have a bank account already. But a bank account is of little benefit if you don't know how to properly manage the money that's in it.

What Is Money Management?

Money management is a way to map out how you will use your money. When you manage your money, you are determining not only how you will spend your money, but also how you will save and invest it. When learning about money management, it's a good idea to start early so that you don't spend beyond your means and end up in debt. If you make smart decisions about your money, you will have money available when you need it.

Unfortunately, though, not everyone knows how to manage money. For instance, in 2012, high school students who took a government-sponsored test on money issues, known as the National Financial Capability Challenge, only got 69 percent of the answers correct. For this reason, parents and educators want to help kids like you manage money effectively.

Why Is Money Management Important?

There are a number of benefits to learning how to manage your money now rather than later. For instance, if you learn how to manage your money effectively, you will:

- Develop good spending and saving habits.
- Learn how to set financial goals and reach them.
- Learn how to make wise purchasing decisions and make your money go further.

- Develop self-control when it comes to making purchases.
- Avoid spending beyond your means and getting into debt.
- Have the ability to give to others in need.

Today, money management is extremely important for teens like you. You have access to more money than ever before. You may earn money from allowances, monetary gifts, chores, and part-time jobs. But money management doesn't just involve the money coming in. It also involves the money going out.

Sometimes you probably would like to have more money on hand. That's where money management can be helpful. With solid money management skills, you will have more money than ever before.

GOOD ¢

Time Is Money

One important concept in money management is the idea that "time is money." What this means is that managing your time along with managing your money is important.

For example, let's assume you make $10 an hour watching your neighbor's kids. If you buy a $30 video game, then you had to work three hours to pay for that game. When you go to purchase the game, your local game store was out of it. But they are expecting more in two days. However, a store an hour away has it in stock. You want it now.

When deciding whether or not to drive the hour there and the hour back to buy the game, you have to consider that time is money. If you drive the hour there and the hour back, you have now paid $50 for the game because of the two hours you spent getting it instead of waiting the two days. Plus, you have to factor in the cost of gasoline.

Be Smart About Money

Dollars and Sense

When it comes to money, you have to realize that other people want it. Some will do almost anything to get it. So do your research before entering contests and buying things, especially online. In fact, online scams are some of the biggest challenges to effective money management. Don't assume that these offers are legitimate. The best practice is to investigate everything first before agreeing to purchase or enter.

NON ¢

Now it's your turn to "Do the Math." The end of each chapter features a math or word problem. Use what you learned in the chapter to help you answer the questions. The right math will help you make the right financial decisions.

Do the Math

Judy makes $12 an hour working at her uncle's hardware store. She has been saving to buy a new iPhone. The cost of the new phone at her local discount store is $300. She has already saved $240. Her cousin tells her that the new iPhone is on sale at a store in the next town for $200. Should Judy drive the half hour one-way to save $100?

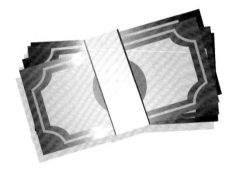

Be Smart About Money

Making Some Dough

Let's face it. Life is expensive. Whether you want the latest clothes, concert tickets, a new cell phone or even a car, it all adds up. Sure, you could put in a lot of overtime at work. Some teens even consider quitting school in order to work full-time. But how much will those extra hours bagging groceries or running a cash register help you in the long run?

Sometimes the smarter answer is to hold off on some of your purchasing instead of logging extra hours at your part-time job or quitting school. Instead, focus on your schoolwork.

That idea might sound lame at first, but you have to think long-term. What do you want your life to be like when you are an adult? Do you want to be scraping by, or do you want to live comfortably?

Diplomas Equal More Dollars

Research shows that high school graduates earn about $8,000 more on average each year than those who don't finish high school, according to the Alliance for Excellent Education. And college

graduates with a bachelor's degree earn $17,800 more on average each year than those with a high school diploma. So holding off on that new iPhone might make sense, especially when you think about where you will be in ten years.

Let's assume you graduate from college when you are twenty-one and start earning money right away. By the time you are thirty-one, you will have made about $178,000 more in those ten years after college than your friends who didn't go at all.

So what's the answer then, when it comes to working? The National Institute for Work and Learning recommends what they call the 10–Hour Technique. In other words, they suggest that teens work only ten hours a week, with most of those hours falling on the weekend.

Another idea is to focus on working full-time in the summer because you don't have to worry about getting your schoolwork done. The key is not to work so much that your grades drop or that you miss homework assignments.

Be Smart About Money

Where Did the Money Go?

There's no greater feeling than receiving a paycheck. After all, you worked hard for that money and now you have plans for it. But, if you are not used to getting a paycheck, the amount on your check can be shocking at first. This amount, called your net pay, is less than what you actually earned. If you're not prepared, it can surprise you.

Net pay is the amount you're paid, or your income, after any deductions. Deductions include things like taxes and insurance, which are subtracted before you get paid. Some deductions are required and some deductions are voluntary. Be sure to make your budget based on your net pay.

Bill Me!

Have you ever heard the old saying "Don't count your chickens before they hatch?" Well, what that means is don't act as if you have something before you actually have it. This is especially true with money. Don't spend your paycheck before you have it in your hand.

Not only is this "bill me" attitude a bad money management practice, but it is also risky. What if something happens and you don't get your paycheck at all? You are still on the hook for everything you spent and now you don't have the money to cover it. It's always a good idea to wait until you have the money in hand before you make any purchases with it. Avoid the "bill me" attitude.

Be Smart About Money

Do the Math

Josh's friend Bill has been working full-time since he graduated from high school. Recently, he was promoted and now is making $20,000 per year. Josh just graduated from college and is making $28,000 per year.

With the new promotion, Bill can now save 30 percent of his paycheck each year, or $6,000. Josh can only save 20 percent (or $5,600) because he has student loans to pay off. His student loans will be paid off in ten years and then he plans to save 30 percent per year (or $8,400).

How much will each friend have in savings in twenty years assuming that both save at the same rate and neither person gets a raise? How much in twenty-five years under the same conditions?

Investing in You

Even though you work and make money, do you sometimes feel like you never have any cash? Are you tempted to work more hours in order to get more money? Maybe you don't need to work more, but instead you need to spend less—or better yet, save more! Saving money is not as much fun as spending it, but it's important, especially when it comes to your financial future.

When you save money, you can use it later to buy things that you want or to pay for bigger ticket items, such as a car or college. Here are some suggestions to get you started on developing a savings plan.

Set Goals. Make saving money just as important as paying bills. Think about your savings goals before you do anything else. For example, do you want a new phone? Are you saving for college? Once you have established your savings goals, don't take on expenses that cut into them. You will always save more money if you make saving money a priority over spending money.

Pay Yourself First. Consider putting 10 to 25 percent of everything you make into a savings account that you plan to let build for a few years. For example, for every $10 you make cutting grass or babysitting, you would immediately put $2.50 into a savings account that you don't touch. Additionally, most savings accounts pay you interest on what you save. Interest is money the bank pays you for allowing them to keep your money.

Have a Strategy. Plan to save a portion of everything you get. This means even saving a little bit from the monetary gifts relatives give you and the money mom and dad give you for doing chores. If you find a way to save a little bit of everything you have coming in, you will save more money over time.

Set Up an Emergency Fund. Make sure that not all the money you are saving is being saved to spend on something in the future. You never know when something unforeseen might happen. When you are an adult, your unforeseen expenses might include car repairs or medical bills. But even teens can have unforeseen expenses. Suppose you borrow a friend's lacrosse equipment and then you lose it. It's your responsibility to replace it. But where will you get the money? If you have been saving correctly, then you should have some money saved that you can use to cover the cost of replacing the equipment.

Be Accountable. Share your savings goals with a parent or another trusted adult. Not only can this person help you stay accountable to your plan, but also he or she may have some additional smart savings ideas.

What Are Your Savings Options?

Now that you know the importance of saving, you can start to consider what method of saving might be best for you. A good first step is to learn about banks and credit unions. Credit unions are member-owned, financial organizations that provide savings, credit, and other financial services to its members.

Sometimes banks and credit unions limit the number of withdrawals you can make or require you to maintain a minimum balance. They also may charge fees for maintaining your account. Shop around until you find the bank or credit union that best fits your needs.

The following are a few places where you can put your money.

Checking Account. When you get a job, it is a good idea to have a checking account. It will be useful not only for paying bills, but also for having your paychecks deposited directly into the account, if your employer offers this option. Checking accounts typically do not pay interest unless you have a large checking account and maintain a high balance. So, it is usually a good idea to keep a little money in your checking account, but to put the bulk of your money in a savings account.

Linking the two accounts together also is a good idea. Then, you can transfer money from your savings to your checking when you need it. When you want to transfer money, or move money from one account to another, you can do this online, at the ATM machine, or at the bank.

An ATM is an automated teller machine that allows you to make bank transactions without a human clerk. Machines are located outside of banks and in shopping malls, stores, and other locations. If you are going to use an ATM to withdraw money or perform other services, be sure you know what fees apply. Some banks charge fees for using their machine, especially if your account is not with them.

Savings Account. A savings account is always a good option for teens because the funds are easily accessible and you earn interest on what you are saving. In most cases, you can withdraw money from a savings account at any time—either from the bank's ATM machine or when the bank is open. You also can transfer money to your checking account if you have one.

When searching for a savings account, be sure the account is FDIC insured. What this means is if the bank goes out of business or mismanages money, the Federal Deposit Insurance Corporation (FDIC) will insure your money up to $250,000.

This makes putting your money in a bank much safer than keeping it in a piggy bank or in a shoebox under your bed.

CD (Certificate of Deposit). A certificate of deposit, or CD, is a type of savings certificate. When you purchase a CD, you are giving a bank your money for a fixed period of time, say six months or a year. In return, you get an interest rate larger than you would from a traditional savings account. It's also a safe way to invest your money and earn interest as long as you choose a CD from a bank that is FDIC insured. Although you can cash in your CD before the end of the specified time period, you may be charged a fee for doing so. Only put money into a CD if you are sure you won't need it until it comes due.

Savings Bonds. U.S. Savings Bonds are investments that are backed by the federal government and offer a safe and easy way for teens to save money. Typically, savings bonds can be purchased electronically through the U.S. Treasury for as little as $25. Bonds accrue value every month and you will always get your money back, unlike other types of investments.

Stock Market. The stock market is a place where buyers and sellers trade companies' stocks for a set price. When you buy stock, then you own part of a company. This part is called a "share." People who own stock are called "shareholders" or "stockholders." When you buy stock in a company, you are hoping the company makes money because then you will receive a share of the profits.

Be Smart About Money

However, if the company you buy stock in loses money, then you don't regain the money you invested.

In the United States, you have to be eighteen years old to open an account that allows you to buy and sell stock.

GOOD ¢

Cut Back, Not Out

One way to save money is to cut back on everyday expenses like candy, drinks, and snacks. For example, let's assume you are spending $6 a week on coffee and snacks. Why not try to cut that in half? Limit yourself to $3 a week for snacks and coffee and save the other $3. In a year, you will have saved more than $150!

NON ¢

Don't Break the Bank!

You've probably heard your parents or others say that some purchases would "break the bank." What this means is that the price was either really high or it would take everything they have saved to purchase it. This is an area where many teens get into trouble. But, if you want to get good at saving, then you should definitely steer clear of purchases that would "break the bank."

Do the Math

Jimmy is fifteen years old and has his first job. He set a goal to save $10 per week and put it in a "rainy-day" fund.

1. If Jimmy saves $10 every week for the next ten years, how much money will he have, not including interest when he is twenty-five?
2. Now that Jimmy is twenty-five, he decides to put the total amount into a six-month CD that earns a flat rate of 3 percent for six months. How much money will he have at the end of six months?

Be Smart About Money

Budgeting Basics

For many people, creating a budget is about as exciting as creating an exercise plan. But it doesn't have to be that way, especially if you have the right attitude. Instead, look at a budget as a way to have more control over your money. It also is a plan that you can use to help you live as well as possible with the money that you have.

One of the first steps in developing a budget is to find out where your money is going. If you are like most teens, you are probably spending your money on clothing, entertainment, food, and drinks.

Dear (Money) Diary

One way to get a handle on how much you are spending is to keep a money diary for two or three months. Once you try it, you might find you actually like keeping track of where your money is going.

There are a number of options for keeping a money diary. Some people prefer to keep a small notebook with them, either

in their backpack or purse, and write down expenses as they occur. Other people prefer a formal method of keeping receipts and logging the amounts into a spreadsheet on the computer. Both methods are effective. Choose one that best fits your style.

Regardless of the method you choose, be sure to write down all the money that comes in. This includes money you get from odd jobs, chores, babysitting, part-time jobs, and gifts. Later, when you are budgeting, this will represent your income.

You also should write down where you spend your money. Be sure you write down everything you can remember. Include the 85¢ you spent at the vending machine and the 25¢ you put into the pencil machine at school. Everything counts and should be recorded.

You also should include the date you spent the money and why you spent it. You will learn a lot from this information. For example, you may find that every Monday you spend money in the vending machine before band practice. Later, when you are budgeting, this may be an expense you can eliminate. One way to avoid this expense is to pack a snack from home, especially if you find you are always hungry at the same time every week.

After keeping track of your spending, make a list of potential cutbacks. Choose areas where you can get by with spending less. Be flexible and make adjustments until you find out what works and what doesn't work.

Be Smart About Money

Using Percentages to Budget

Once you have a handle on where you are spending money, try developing an initial budget. One easy way to budget is to use the percentages method. The percentages method means you take your net pay and set aside percentages of it for savings and to pay for certain things. Most experts recommend saving a minimum of 10 percent of your income each month before determining expenses. But if you can save more, do it! The idea is to pick percentages that will work for you.

Here is an example of a percentage budget. You want to save at least 30 percent of your income each month because you want to build an emergency fund and save for college. But you also want to buy a new cell phone in about four or five months, so you need to save for that, too. So that's another 20 percent you plan to save each month. Finally, you like to give at least 10 percent of your income each month to your favorite charity. That will leave you 40 percent to spend on everyday expenses and entertainment.

Using the percentages mentioned earlier, let's figure out how to budget your money. In this example, you have $300 coming in each month from odd jobs, chores, and your part-time job. As a result, you would save $90 per month ($300 × .30) to build your emergency fund and to save for college. Ideally, this money would not be touched.

You also would have $120 per month to spend on everyday expenses, such as food, clothing, entertainment, and

transportation ($300 × .40). This $120 per month averages to about $30 per week or just over $4 per day. Some days you will spend more than others, but knowing about how much you have a day to spend will help you keep control of your spending.

As for the rest of your income, you would have $30 to give to your favorite charity each month ($300 × .10) and $60 ($300 × .20) to put away each month for the new cell phone you want to purchase in four or five months. Saving $60 per month for four months would give you $240 for a new phone.

The key to developing a budget using the percentages method is to be sure it works for you. If the budget isn't working, revise it until you find a plan that feels right to you. Try not to cut savings in order to balance your budget.

Using a Line–Item Budget

With a line-item budget, you list all your income and all your expenses, line by line. When listing expenses, you will have two categories. One category will include fixed expenses, which are unavoidable expenses. Examples include rent, utilities, car insurance, gasoline, and loan payments. As a teen, you may not have all of these expenses until you are older. But the idea is to consider what you have to pay every month. Ideally, savings is included in your fixed expenses, especially if you make paying yourself first a priority.

Your second expense category includes adjustable expenses, which are expenses that can be cut or adjusted if necessary.

Be Smart About Money

Examples include food, clothing, entertainment, cell phones, household supplies, and personal care.

With this type of budget, you will use your money diary to fill in the average cost that you spend on specific items each month. For example, if you spent $100 on clothing one month, nothing on clothing in the second month, and $20 on clothing the third month, you are spending an average of $40 per month on clothing. (e.g. $100 + $0 + $20=$120 ... $120/3 months = $40). You would put $40 per month under clothing in your line item budget.

Make Adjustments

Whether you are using the percentages method or the line-item method, you need to address budget shortfalls. These occur when your spending is greater than your income. Try to be creative when it comes to cutting back.

Effective budgeting is one of the most important aspects of money management. Not only does it help you handle your spending, but it also helps you meet your financial and savings goals. You may find that effective budgeting can reduce worries about having enough money.

Making a Wish List

After devising a budget, consider
creating a "wish list" of things you want
or need but can't afford right now. Then,
make a goal to save for at least one "wish list" item.

For example, maybe you would like to buy some
software for your personal computer. The cost of
the software is $50. After you look at your budget,
you realize that you can save $5 a week by cutting
out a few unnecessary snacks and treats. By saving
$5 per week, you will be able to buy the new
software in just two and a half months.

Wants or Needs?

One mistake teens make when it comes
to spending is confusing wants and
needs. For example, you need clothing
but you don't need a $50 pair of jeans. The $50
jeans are a want. Likewise, you need water to
survive. But you don't need a $2.50 bottle of water
when the drinking fountain is just down the hall.
Remember, a need is something you cannot do
without. A want, on the other hand, is something
you would like to have but is not necessary. If you
confuse the two, budgeting will be a challenge.

Be Smart About Money

Do the Math

Part I.
Julie's budget doesn't balance. She is $25 over budget. Show her where she could "cut back but not out" in order to make her budget balance.

Income:

$300 per month (from allowance and babysitting)

Total Income   **$300 per month**

Fixed Expenses:

Savings	$20 per month
Cell Phone	$70 per month
Transportation	$30 per month
Subtotal	**$120 per month**

Adjustable Expenses:

Starbucks	$20 per month
Entertainment	$50 per month
Clothing	$100 per month
Books	$20 per month
Manicure	$15 per month
Subtotal	**$205 per month**

Total Income   **$300 – $325 = –$25.00**

Part II.
Next, try creating your own monthly budget. Try to determine where you can save money each month.

Getting Financially Fit

Money. You probably feel like you have a lifetime to earn it, save it, and spend it. But if you want to make the most of every penny you have, you should start today getting yourself into financial shape. One way to get in financial shape is to become a better consumer.

You Better Shop Around

You live in a world where the pressure to buy things and spend money is constant. You are bombarded by ads on TV and on the computer. But if you want to be good at managing money, you have to learn to resist these temptations. Focusing on becoming a smart shopper is key to effective money management. Here are some tips.

- **Resist impulse buys**. Wait a few days and see if you still really want it.
- **Don't shop for entertainment**. When you shop because you have nothing else to do, you will end up buying things you don't need.

- **Shop sales**. If you buy things you need when they are on sale, you will save money. But don't buy something you don't need just because it's on sale.
- **Be a smart consumer.** Research big purchases like computers and cell phones on the Internet. Not only can you compare prices, but you also can read consumer reviews and find out if the product is really one you want.

Using the Right Tools

Another way to get financially fit is to understand the money tools you have available to you and use them wisely. Aside from cash, there are three different ways you can pay for things, including personal checks, debit cards, and credit cards.

Personal Checks. Personal checks are checks you write from your checking account to pay bills or make purchases. Many banks also allow you to write electronic checks. These are checks that the bank sends on your behalf when you enter the information online. For example, if you need to pay your cell-phone bill, you may be able to enter your account information online and write a check directly from your checking account. This saves time and money on postage. Be sure you know if your bank charges a fee for this service before using it.

Here are some tips for using personal checks:

- **Record all transactions in your check register.** You need to keep track of what you are spending so that you can avoid overdrawing your account. Every time you write a check,

money is deducted from the account. This reduces the amount of money you have available to you to make purchases.

- **Know your balance.** Before writing a check, it's important that you know the balance in your account. This balance is not the available balance shown online. It is the balance in your check register. You want to be careful not to overdraw your account.

- **Consider whether a check is your best option.** Sometimes, when you write a check, the cashier will need to record a lot of personal information on your check. Then, this information travels everywhere your check travels. Some money experts feel it is safer to use a debit card for purchases because there is less personal information shared.

Debit Cards. Debit cards look like credit cards but function differently. They are tied to a bank account and allow you to spend up to the amount in the bank account. Your spending limit is determined by the amount in the bank account. Here are some things to remember about debit cards:

- **Record all transactions in your check register.** You need to keep track of what you are spending so that you can avoid overdrawing your account. Debit cards are not a source of free money. Your debit card is linked to your bank account. Every time you make a purchase, money is deducted from the account.

- **Know your balance.** Before using a debit card to make purchases, it is important that you know the balance in

Be Smart About Money

your account. This balance is not the available balance shown on an ATM receipt. It is the balance in your check register. If you use your debit card and you still have checks that haven't cleared the bank, you could overdraw your account. As a result, all your outstanding checks would bounce, which will result in return check fees.

- **Remember your money supply is limited.** It's important to think through purchases. Use your savings goals and your budget to help determine if you should make a purchase.

Credit Cards. There are three types of credit cards. These include bank cards, such as Visa and MasterCard, general credit cards like American Express, and proprietary cards like cards for Old Navy, The Gap, and Target.

These cards can be tempting for someone who likes to shop. That's why good money management skills are required. If you misuse credit cards, you can damage your credit history and create a mountain of debt.

Digging out from credit-card debt can be difficult and time-consuming. So don't use credit cards unless you have the discipline to pay them on time and stay within credit limits. If you don't follow those guidelines, you could end up paying extra fees or higher interest rates. What's more, late or missed payments will damage your credit history. This may not seem like a big deal now, but it can affect your ability to buy a car or get a loan in the future.

Fortunately, most credit-card companies require that teens be at least eighteen years old to have a card in their name. But sometimes parents will cosign for a credit card. When a parent cosigns, this means that he or she is responsible for the debt. So if you don't pay your credit-card bill, your parent will be responsible to pay it.

Here are some things to remember about credit cards:

- **Use credit cards for convenience only.** Because credit cards typically have high interest rates, it is usually a good idea to use them only when it is convenient like when ordering books or concert tickets online. But pay attention to your budget and your savings goals before using a credit card. If you know you are not able to pay off the bill when it arrives, then this is a warning sign that you may be spending more than you can afford.

- **Credit cards are not extra income**. Using credit doesn't give you more money to spend. When you use credit to buy something and you do not pay off the balance in full every month, you will pay interest. This means that you are paying more for everything you purchase.

- **Avoid making minimum payments**. Credit-card companies allow for minimum payments because they make money when you choose that option. Remember, the longer you take to pay, the more it costs you in interest. Additionally, it takes many years to pay off a credit-card balance if you only make minimum payments.

Be Smart About Money

Helping Others

Once you are in good financial shape, then you have more flexibility with your money. One option for this newfound freedom is being able to help others. Research shows that people who give generously of their time and money get tremendous amounts of satisfaction. They also have a better appreciation of what they have.

If you are interested in helping others, consider donating money to a charity you admire. You also could ask friends and relatives to donate to a charity of your choice instead of giving you holiday or birthday gifts.

You also can donate your time. Join an organization at your school or in your community that helps others. Or, help your parents when they volunteer their time.

Cha-Ching!

One mistake young people often
make when saving for bigger items
is forgetting to factor in sales tax. Sales tax,
which is sometimes referred to as retail sales
tax, is charged for consumption of goods and
services. Usually, you have to pay this tax when
you purchase things. In other words, if you are
planning to purchase a video game for $49.99,
you actually need to take more than that to the
store. The percentage of sales tax varies from area
to area, but let's assume your local sales tax is
7 percent. Your $49.99 video game would actually
cost you $53.49. ($49.99 × .07 = $3.50 (rounded
up)—$49.99 + $3.50 = $53.49). Don't forget about
sales tax and arrive at the store with a $50 bill. You
will be embarrassed when the cashier tells you
that you don't have enough money.

Be Smart About Money

Do the Math

Jennifer is looking forward to the sale at her local department store. The ad says that everything in the store is 35 percent off. Her local sales tax rate is 6.5 percent. Jennifer falls in love with a bag with a price tag of $75. What will the total cost of the bag be?

Know the Score

Chapter 6

How you manage money says a lot about you—especially when it comes to your credit report. A credit report contains very detailed information about your ability to manage money, be responsible, and pay bills on time.

A credit report also includes previous addresses, your social security number, current and previous employers, and an estimated income. Additionally, it tracks your payment history and supplies this information to those who request it. These businesses then use this report to determine if they want to do business with you.

It also contains detailed information about each credit-card account you own. For example, it will show the type of account, the balance you owe, and your payment history. It is this information that credit-reporting agencies use to assign you a credit score. A credit score is like a grade that tells others how good you are at managing money. It also determines the rate of interest you will pay on any future loans.

It's a good idea to know what your credit report says. As a consumer, you are entitled to a free copy of your credit report

Be Smart About Money

every twelve months. Go to the Federal Trade Commission (FTC) Web site for information on getting a free credit report.

Protecting Your Credit History

You've probably heard your parents talk about "identity theft." Maybe you have heard about people pretending to be someone they are not on Facebook. Identity theft occurs when a person's identity is stolen and used without permission. Criminals use this personal information to withdraw money from accounts, purchase things, and open credit cards.

Most people think kids are safe from identity theft. Actually, you are more at risk. Kids are fifty-one times more likely to have their identities stolen than adults, according to a study done by Carnegie Mellon University.

Criminals often target young people like you even though you may be too young to apply for a credit card. They use your name, address, and social security number to open accounts because the credit history is clean. Here are some ideas for protecting yourself:

- **Keep your information private.** Be careful with your full name, address, phone number, date of birth, and even your mother's maiden name. You also should not share your social security number with anyone—especially online or over the telephone.
- **Watch what you do online.** It's never a good idea to give out personal information online or to post it on a social networking site, such as Facebook, Twitter, or Google Plus.

- **Keep it locked up.** Keep important documents, such as your birth certificate or documents with your social security number, in a secure place like your parents' safe deposit box or a safe at home.
- **Be stingy with passwords and ID numbers.** It's never a good idea to share your passwords or ID numbers with friends, no matter how much you trust them.
- **Keep your cell phone and other electronics password protected.** Always keep your phone, e-mail accounts, and even your computer password protected.

Give Yourself Credit

According to a study by the JumpStart Coalition for Financial Literacy, 31.8 percent of high school seniors use a credit card. About half of these students have a card in their names. The rest use cards issued in a parent's name. The rate of credit-card usage jumps significantly by the time teens become freshmen in college. But using a credit card is not as simple as swiping it at the cash register. Teens have to be sure they can handle the responsibility.

Having a solid credit history is important. Some utility companies, such as the cable company or the telephone company, may pull your credit report before allowing you to have an account. In addition, some apartment and property managers will pull your credit report before allowing you to rent from them. Some employers will pull a credit report before hiring you. A bad credit report can work against you as you look for a job because

Be Smart About Money

employers often decide if you are a responsible person by looking at this report.

Remember, using credit requires that you have the discipline to pay on time and stay within credit limits. So if you don't have the money to pay off your credit-card bill when it's due, then don't use the credit card.

By learning how to use credit wisely, you will be on your way to making good financial decisions. Every effective money management plan starts with saving and ends with avoiding debt problems.

Extra Credit

Whether or not you should get a credit card depends on your level of self-control. You need to be able to keep purchases at a minimum. You also need discipline to pay off the balance every month. Using a credit card should be done only to build your credit rating. Using a credit card as a source of emergency funds is never a good idea.

When you use a credit card, you really are taking out a loan with the bank. And if you don't pay off the balance when it's due, you will be paying high interest rates. These rates end up costing you money.

The Big Three

Teens make three common mistakes when they get a credit card. These include:

1. **Not using a credit card wisely**. Knowing how to use a credit card is one of the keys to good money management. First, you should never use a credit card for extra cash. If you don't have the money to pay off the balance when it comes due, you should not use a credit card. Second, if you use a credit card only when you can pay off the balance when it comes due, then you can leave your money in a savings account to earn more interest.

2. **Not paying your bills on time.** If you pay your bills late, you will quickly damage your credit score. Setting up an automatic payment from your checking account can help keep you on track and can make bill paying easier.

3. **Paying only the minimum amount due.** Paying the full balance on time will build a good credit history. You do not have to carry a balance on your credit card to build a credit history. Keep in mind, that the longer you take to pay off your debt, the more it will cost you.

Be Smart About Money

Do the Math

Melanie receives an e-mail saying that the bank she does business with needs her to update her records. The e-mail asks her to provide her social security number, address, birthday, and her bank account number so that there is no interruption in her banking. Melanie provides the information they requested right away because she doesn't want her checks to bounce. Did Melanie do the right thing? Explain.

Glossary

ATM—An automated teller machine that allows you to make bank transactions without a human clerk; machines are located outside of banks and in shopping malls, stores, and other locations.

budget—A plan that you can use to help you have more control over your money.

credit card—Allows the cardholder to pay for goods and services based on the holder's promise to pay for them; consumers also are allowed to carry a continuing balance and pay interest on what they have charged.

credit report—A record of an individual's past borrowing and repaying history, including information about late payments and bankruptcy.

credit union—Member-owned, financial organizations that provide savings, credit, and other financial services to its members.

debit card—Looks like a credit card but is tied to a bank account and allows you to spend up to the amount in the bank account.

Be Smart About Money

debt—An obligation owed by one party (the debtor) to a second party (the creditor).

deductions—Taxes, insurance, and other expenses that are subtracted from your check before you get paid; some deductions are required and some deductions are voluntary.

identity theft—This occurs when a person's identity is stolen and used without permission; criminals use personal information to withdraw money from accounts, purchase things, and open credit cards.

interest—The return earned on an investment, or the fee charged by a lender for the use of borrowed money, usually expressed as an annual percentage.

money management—A way to map out how you will use your money by determining not only how you will spend your money, but also how you will save and invest it.

net pay—The amount you're paid, or your income, after any deductions; the amount you should use when formulating a budget.

personal check—A check written from your checking account to pay bills or make purchases; it can be from a paper checkbook or in the form of an electronic check written online.

Learn More

Books

Bellenir, Karen, ed. *Cash and Credit Information for Teens: Tips for a Successful Financial Life*. Detroit: Omnigraphics, 2009.

Butler, Tamsen. *The Complete Guide to Personal Finance: For Teenagers*. Ocala, Fla.: Atlantic Publishing Group, 2010.

Chatzky, Jean. *Not Your Parents' Money Book: Making, Saving, and Spending Your Own Money*. New York: Simon and Schuster Books for Young Readers, 2010.

Donovan, Sandy. *Budgeting Smarts: How to Set Goals, Save Money, Spend Wisely, and More*. Minneapolis, Minn.: Twenty-First Century Books, 2012.

Internet Addresses

Junior Achievement Student Center
   <http://studentcenter.ja.org/Pages/default.aspx>

The Mint.org: Fun Financial Literacy Activities
   <http://themint.org>

MyMoney.gov
   <http://www.mymoney.gov/index.html>

Be Smart About Money

Do the Math Answer Key

Chapter 1: Money Matters
Yes. She makes $12 an hour. So driving one hour would only cost her $12 plus the cost of gas. Because $12 is significantly less than the $100 she will save, it still saves her money to drive the extra hour to get the phone at a cheaper price.

Chapter 2: Making Some Dough
Bill will save $120,000 in 20 years and $150,000 in 25 years.
($6,000 \times 20 = 120,000$; $6,000 \times 5 = 30,000$; $120,000 + 30,000 = 150,000$)
Josh will save $140,000 in 20 years and $182,000 in 25 years.
($5,600 \times 10 = 56,000$; $8,400 \times 10 = 84,000$; $84,000 + 56,000 = 140,000$
$8,400 \times 5 = 42,000$; $140,000 + 42,000 = 182,000$)

Chapter 3: Investing in You
1. 52 weeks in a year $\times$ 10 years $= 520$ weeks; $\$10.00 \times 520 = \$5,200$;
2. $\$5,200 \times .03 = \$156$; $\$156 + \$5,200 = \$5,356.00$

Chapter 4: Budgeting Basics
Possible answer to Part I is to subtract $5 from each line item under adjustable expenses . . . or deduct more from clothing since she spends so much each month. Any combination is correct as long as the budget balances and nothing has been cut out. Do not touch the fixed expenses.

Chapter 5: Getting Financially Fit
$\$75.00 \times .35 = \$26.25$; $\$75.00 - \$26.25 = \$48.75$; $\$48.75 \times .065 = \$3.17$ (rounded); $\$48.75 + \$3.17 = \$51.92$

Chapter 6: Know the Score
Possible answer: No. You should never provide your personal information through an e-mail, even if the e-mail looks legitimate. Melanie should have called her bank instead and asked if there was a problem.

Index

Be Smart About Money

What makes YOU a Michigan kid?

What do you like to do on a snowy day?

X·ING

Michigan Maple Syrup...YUM!

Did you know that it takes 40 gallons of maple sap to make 1 gallon of syrup? Learn more about Michigan's maple syrup producers by visiting Vermontville's annual Maple Syrup Festival held each year in April.

Here are some treats you can make with maple syrup!

Michigan Maple Fudge

- 2 cups maple syrup
- 1 tablespoon light corn syrup
- 1 cup cream
- 1 cup nuts (optional)

Combine maple syrup, corn syrup, and cream in a saucepan over low heat. Cook until soft-ball stage, or when a candy thermometer inserted into the mixture reads 235°F–240°F. Remove from heat and beat until mixture thickens. If using nuts, stir them in now. Pour into a greased pan. Let cool completely before cutting into pieces.

Snow Candy

You only need two ingredients to make Snow Candy:

- clean, fresh snow
- maple syrup

Fill a bowl or pie tin with clean, fresh snow. Boil maple syrup for about 4 or 5 minutes. Carefully pour the hot syrup over the snow in ribbons. Almost immediately, the syrup will harden into a taffy-like candy. After a few seconds, your Snow Candy will be cool enough to handle and eat!

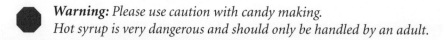

Warning: Please use caution with candy making. Hot syrup is very dangerous and should only be handled by an adult.

DRAW!

Today's date: _____

WRITE!

Today's date: _____

Now, write your own poem here:

1st Stanza

I am _____

I wonder _____

I hear _____

I see _____

I want _____

I am _____

2nd Stanza

I pretend _____

I feel _____

I touch _____

I worry _____

I cry _____

I am _____

3rd Stanza

I understand _____

I say _____

I dream _____

I try _____

I hope _____

I am _____

Can you write your own poem? Here's how.

1st Stanza

I am............................ (*two special characteristics you have*)

I wonder .... (*something you are actually curious about*)

I hear .... (*an imaginary sound*)

I see.. (*an imaginary sight*)

I want...(*an actual desire*)

I am............................. (*the first line of the poem repeated*)

2nd Stanza

I pretend .... (*something you actually pretend to do*)

I feel .... (*a feeling about something imaginary*)

I touch... (*an imaginary touch*)

I worry .... (*something that really bothers you*)

I cry.............................. (*something that makes you very sad*)

I am.............................. (*the first line of the poem repeated*)

3rd Stanza

I understand .... (*something you know is true*)

I say... (*something you believe in*)

I dream........................ (*something you actually dream about*)

I try.................... (*something you really make an effort about*)

I hope............................... (*something you actually hope for*)

I am.............................. (*the first line of the poem repeated*)

DRAW!

Today's date: _____

WRITE!

Today's date: _____

_____

_____

_____

_____

_____

_____

_____

_____

_____

_____

_____

_____

_____

_____

_____

_____

_____

_____

_____

If I could change one thing
about where I live it would be

_____

_____

_____

_____

_____

_____

_____

_____

A place I hope to go someday

_____

_____

If I could live anywhere in the world I'd choose

_____

_____

Someone I wish lived near me

_____

_____

Of all the places I've been, I liked this best

_____

_____

Of all the places I've been, I really didn't like

_____

_____

DRAW!

Today's date: _____

WRITE!

Today's date: _____

_____

_____

_____

_____

_____

_____

_____

_____

_____

_____

_____

_____

_____

_____

_____

_____

_____

_____

WRITE!

Today's date: _____

_____

_____

_____

_____

_____

_____

_____

_____

_____

_____

_____

_____

_____

_____

_____

_____

_____

_____

_____

School days

My favorite subject in school

_____

_____

_____

My least favorite subject in school

_____

_____

_____

If I were a teacher, I would

_____

_____

_____

If I could change one thing about school, I would

_____

_____

_____

The thing I like most about school

_____

_____

_____

What do you love about going
back to school?

SCHOOL BUS
STOP

DRAW!

Today's date: _____

WRITE!

Today's date: _____

_____

_____

_____

_____

_____

_____

_____

_____

_____

_____

_____

_____

_____

_____

_____

_____

_____

_____

My least favorite thing about today was

_____

_____

_____

_____

_____

_____

_____

Would I visit here again? Why or why not?

_____

_____

_____

_____

_____

_____

Today we went to

_____

_____

_____

_____

My favorite thing about today was

_____

_____

_____

_____

_____

_____

_____

DRAW!

Today's date: _____

WRITE!

Today's date: _____

If I made a movie, it would be about

_____

_____

If I made a TV show, it would be about

_____

_____

If I could star in a movie, I would star as a

_____

_____

If I could star in a TV show, I would star as a

_____

_____

I think it would be fun to be an actor because

_____

_____

If I wrote a book it would be about

_____

_____

_____

_____

_____

_____

_____

_____

_____

_____

DRAW!

Today's date: _____

WRITE!

Today's date: _____

_____

_____

_____

_____

_____

_____

_____

_____

_____

_____

_____

_____

_____

_____

_____

_____

_____

_____

_____

_____

A place I hope to go someday

When I grow up I want to be

DRAW!

Today's date: _____

WRITE!

Today's date: _____

_____

_____

_____

_____

_____

_____

_____

_____

_____

_____

_____

_____

_____

_____

_____

_____

_____

_____

Outside and Inside S'mores

You'll need

Marshmallows
Graham crackers, broken in halves
Chocolate bars, broken in halves
A long stick or skewer for campfire s'mores, or
a baking sheet and aluminum foil for indoor s'mores

HOW TO MAKE CAMPFIRE S'MORES

Get your graham crackers and chocolate ready first.
Lay a chocolate bar half on one graham cracker half and have another
graham cracker half ready to go. Now put a marshmallow on the end of
your stick and hold over the fire, turning to keep it browning nicely and
evenly on all sides. It's finished when it's brown all over and a little crispy
on the outside. Now have a friend sandwich the marshmallow between
the graham and chocolate halves while you pull your stick out of the
marshmallow. Now you have a s'more!

HOW TO MAKE S'MORES IN THE OVEN

Heat oven to 350 degrees. Line a baking sheet with foil.
Lay cracker halves on baking sheet, top with chocolate bar halves,
then marshmallows.
Toast in oven for about 5 minutes, just until marshmallow is melty
and chocolate begins to soften.
Remove from oven and top with another graham cracker half.
S'mores indoors all year round!

Let's go CAMPING!

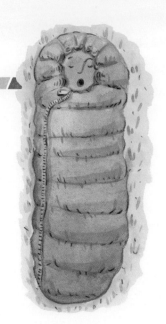

Have you ever gone camping? You can go camping in your own backyard. If it's too cold to camp outside, how about camping in your living room? You can even make s'mores in the kitchen oven!

Write about your camping experiences, or where you hope to go camping someday.

DRAW!

Today's date: _____

WRITE!

Today's date: _____

_____

_____

_____

_____

_____

_____

_____

_____

_____

_____

_____

_____

_____

_____

_____

_____

_____

_____

My least favorite thing about today was

Would I visit here again? Why or why not?

Today we went to

_____

_____

_____

_____

My favorite thing about today was

_____

_____

_____

_____

_____

_____

_____

DRAW!

Today's date: _____

WRITE!

Today's date: _____

_____

_____

_____

_____

_____

_____

_____

_____

_____

_____

_____

_____

_____

_____

_____

_____

Can you think of some of your own fun games to play?

_____

_____

_____

_____

_____

_____

_____

_____

Let's play MORE GAMES!

Billboard Poetry

1. Take turns choosing four words from road signs.
2. Give those words to another player who will have one minute to turn the words into a four-line rhyming poem using one word per line.

Eating the Alphabet Game

To start, the first player says, "I'm so hungry I could eat an apple" (or anteater, or alligator). The second player then has to choose something beginning with the next letter of the alphabet, adding to the first player's choice: "I'm so hungry I could eat an apple and a balloon," and so on. See if your family can make it to Z, with each player remembering all the items that came before: "apple, balloon...zebra!"

What is your favorite food?

_____

_____

_____

_____

DRAW!

Today's date: _____

WRITE!

Today's date: _____

_____

_____

_____

_____

_____

_____

_____

_____

_____

_____

_____

_____

_____

_____

_____

_____

My least favorite thing about today was

_____

_____

_____

_____

_____

_____

_____

Would I visit here again? Why or why not?

_____

_____

_____

_____

_____

Today we went to

My favorite thing about today was

DRAW!

Today's date: _____

WRITE!

Today's date: _____

_____

_____

_____

_____

_____

_____

_____

_____

_____

_____

_____

_____

_____

_____

_____

_____

_____

My least favorite thing about today was

GOOD LUCK

25 MPH

Would I visit here again? Why or why not?

Today we went to

_____

_____

_____

_____

My favorite thing about today was

_____

_____

_____

_____

_____

_____

_____

_____

_____

_____

_____

DRAW!

Today's date: _____

WRITE!

Today's date: _____

_____

_____

_____

_____

_____

_____

_____

_____

_____

_____

_____

_____

_____

_____

_____

_____

Favorite movie

Favorite TV show

Favorite video game

Favorite book

Favorite art projects

When it rains,
my favorite things to do:

DRAW!

Today's date: _____

WRITE!

Today's date: _____

_____

_____

_____

_____

_____

_____

_____

_____

_____

_____

_____

_____

_____

_____

_____

_____

_____

_____

...Now...Let's COOK something!

Making a homemade pizza!

FOR YOUR CRUST:

You can use your favorite pizza-dough recipe, or a store-bought pizza crust, or even English muffin halves or tortillas for your crust.

MAKING FRESH PIZZA SAUCE:

Wash and cut as many tomatoes as you like into chunks.
Wash and dry a good handful each of basil and oregano, and chop.

In a saucepan over medium heat, sauté chopped onion and garlic in a small amount of butter or vegetable oil. If you like your sauce spicy, add crushed red pepper next. Now add the tomatoes and herbs and allow the mixture to come to a boil. Turn down the heat to a simmer, stirring occasionally, and let the sauce simmer until most of the liquid has cooked out.

Take sauce off the stove and use either a container blender or a hand-held blender to purée the sauce. Put sauce back on the heat, let it come to a boil again, then allow to simmer until it is the consistency you like.

Let it cool, then spread on pizza dough, or store in the fridge for another time.

ASSEMBLING YOUR PIZZA:

Spread sauce over pizza dough. Top with your chopped, fresh-picked peppers, and any other fresh veggies or meats you like.
Now sprinkle cheese over everything and bake in the oven according to your pizza dough recipe. Yum! A home-grown pizza!

Let's GROW something!

Grow a Pizza Garden!

Start plants indoors in early spring, then transfer to pots or the ground outside once they've sprouted and there is no longer danger of frost.

You'll need to grow:

HERBS:

  • Basil and Oregano

VEGETABLES for SAUCE and TOPPINGS:

  • Tomatoes and Bell peppers

What is your very favorite kind of pizza?

_____

_____

_____

_____

_____

_____

DRAW!

Today's date: _____

WRITE!

Today's date: _____

My least favorite thing about today was

Would I visit here again? Why or why not?

Today we went to

_____

_____

_____

_____

My favorite thing about today was

_____

_____

_____

_____

_____

_____

_____

_____

_____

_____

DRAW!

Today's date: _____

WRITE!

Today's date: _____

_____

_____

_____

_____

_____

_____

_____

_____

_____

_____

_____

_____

_____

_____

_____

_____

_____

_____

License Plate Game

Make a list of all the states. See how many different state license plates you can find, and check them off your list. (Variation: Keep a list of all the vanity plates you find.)

Make up your own funny license plates.

Auto Tag

Each person chooses a symbol or something you are likely to encounter regularly on the road, such as a gas station logo, a restaurant sign, a farm animal, a motorcycle. When a player sees her item, she calls it out and gently tags the next player, who then proceeds to search for his symbol, and so on.

Let's play some games!

Going on a trip?

Here are some fun games to play on your next road trip.

Scavenger Hunt

Before you start out on your trip, make a list of items and places you might see along the way (11 blue cars, 2 bridges, 5 motels, 3 towns that start with the letter M, etc.). Check them off as you find them.

What is the funniest town name you've ever heard?

_____

_____

_____

_____

_____

If you were going to name a town, what would it be?

_____

_____

DRAW!

Today's date: _____

WRITE!

Today's date: _____

_____

_____

_____

_____

_____

_____

_____

_____

_____

_____

_____

_____

_____

_____

_____

_____

_____

_____

Where is the "Cereal Bowl of America?" You guessed it! Michigan!

Battle Creek, home of the Kellogg's company, is often called the "Cereal Bowl of America." Battle Creek produces more cereal than any other city in the world!

Do you have a favorite cereal?

_____

_____

Michigan Motor Mix

Ingredients:

- 1 cup dry cereal
- 1 cup dried cherries
- 1 cup dried apples

Toss in zip-top bag, shake to combine.

Variations: try popcorn or pretzels instead of cereal, try different types of cereal, add nuts or chocolate pieces, or any combination of your favorite dried fruits.

DRAW!

Today's date: _____

WRITE!

Today's date: _____

Apples are the largest fruit crop grown in Michigan. There are apple festivals held all over Michigan in September and October.

Have you ever been apple picking?

_____

_____

_____

What is your favorite apple recipe?

_____

_____

_____

_____

What do cherries and apples have in common?
Michigan!

Michigan produces more red tart cherries than any other state in the US! To celebrate, Traverse City, the "Cherry Capital of the World," holds the National Cherry Festival each July.

What is your favorite cherry recipe?

_____

_____

_____

_____

_____

_____

_____

_____

_____

DRAW!

Today's date: _____

WRITE!

Today's date: _____

_____

_____

_____

_____

_____

_____

_____

_____

_____

_____

_____

_____

_____

_____

_____

_____

_____

_____

My least favorite thing about today was

_____

_____

_____

_____

_____

_____

_____

_____

Would I visit here again? Why or why not?

_____

_____

_____

_____

_____

Today we went to

_____

_____

_____

_____

My favorite thing about today was

_____

_____

_____

_____

_____

_____

_____

_____

_____

_____

_____

DRAW!

Today's date: _____

WRITE!

Today's date: _____

_____

_____

_____

_____

_____

_____

_____

_____

_____

_____

_____

_____

_____

_____

_____

_____

_____

State fossil:

State fish:

State wildflower:

State stone:

State tree:

State nickname:

The great state of Michigan!

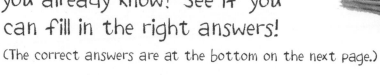

Are you a Michigan kid?
How many state facts do
you already know? See if you
can fill in the right answers!
(The correct answers are at the bottom on the next page.)

State mammal:

_____

State flower:

_____

State bird:

_____

State reptile:

_____

State gem:

_____

DRAW!

Today's date: _____

WRITE!

Today's date: _____

Lake Superior
Canada
Houghton
Marquette
Sault Ste. Marie
Escanaba
Wisconsin
Mackinaw City
Lake Michigan
Lake Huron
Petoskey
Alpena
Traverse City
Higgins Lake
Cadillac
Ludington
Bay City
Saginaw
Muskegon
Grand Rapids
Port Huro
Flint
Lansing
Detroit
Ann Arbor
Battle Creek
Kalamazoo
Lake Erie
Where Do YOU Live?
Illinois
Indiana
Ohio

Where do you live in Michigan?

Your address, town/city, and phone number:

_____

_____

_____

Can you walk to school from your house?

_____

_____

How far away do your friends live from you?

_____

_____

_____

Do you have any parks nearby?

_____

_____

_____

Your favorite thing about your neighborhood is...

_____

_____

_____

Diary of a Michigan Kid

Artwork by Cyd Moore

Sleeping Bear Press™

315 E. Eisenhower Parkway, Suite 200
Ann Arbor MI 48108
www.sleepingbearpress.com

© 2010 Sleeping Bear Press is an imprint of Gale, a part of Cengage Learning.

10 9 8 7 6 5 4 3 2 1

ISBN 978-1-58536-523-4

Printed by China Translation & Printing Services Limited, Guangdong Province, China. 1st printing. 05/2010

My name is

_____

I am _____ years old

and in _____ grade

My best friend is

_____

I live in Michigan: yes   no

I have lived here for_____